TEQUILA MADE ME DO IT

TEQUILA MADE ME DO IT

60 TANTALIZING TEQUILA AND MEZCAL COCKTAILS

CECILIA RIOS MURRIETA

ILLUSTRATED BY RUBY TAYLOR

Andrews McMeel
PUBLISHING®

Andrews McMeel Publishing
a division of Andrews McMeel Universal
1130 Walnut Street, Kansas City, Missouri 64106

www.andrewsmcmeel.com

19 20 21 22 23 HPL 10 9 8 7 6 5 4 3 2 1

ISBN: 978-1-4494-9971-6

Library of Congress Control Number: 2019934290

ATTENTION: SCHOOLS AND BUSINESSES

Andrews McMeel books are available at quantity discounts with bulk purchase for educational, business, or sales promotional use. For information, please e-mail the Andrews McMeel Publishing Special Sales Department: specialsales@amuniversal.com.

CONTENTS

INTRODUCTION

It only took one sip, and the world was smitten. Mexico, the land that not only gave us mariachis, chocolate, *chilaquiles,* and *chapulines*, also gave the world the gift of agave. Most people have heard of tequila, but mezcal and bacanora are also among the now Protected Designations of Origin that exist within the Mexican territory. With a history spanning over 400 years, agave spirits, once an obscure category within the realm of alcohol, have now become the talk of the town in a globalized world thirsty for adventure and craft.

For decades, people have associated tequila with a raucous weekend in Cabo, and mezcal with a creepy crawler at the bottom of the bottle. These associations created an unpopular image of agave spirits that did a huge disservice to the intricate process and sophistication behind the distillation of the agave plant. Today, thanks to an increased awareness of the individuality and craft behind the products we consume, the world has embarked on a journey through Mexico and its spirits. Tequila and mezcal have fought an arduous battle to gain the recognition they now have from some of the top bartenders and drinks experts around the world. These spirits take us back to the traditional roots and folklore of Mexican culture. Beyond simply becoming a trend, they have managed to maintain their traditional character and to establish themselves as a distinct and respected category within the world of spirits.

From the Classic Margarita (page 23) to the Disco & Vine (page 140), tequila and mezcal shine from center stage in both classic staples and innovative creations garnered from swanky cocktail bars and old-school cantinas across the globe. Sipped neat, paired with a playful Sangrita (page 48), or shaken in a classic cocktail, the character and notes of agave, ranging from fruity and vegetal to spicy and floral, will captivate even the most skeptical drinker. It can be intimidating to venture into a seemingly foreign world of drinks that has the added stigma of being shot back with lime and salt. However, once you take the plunge into the world of agave, you will find complexity and superiority reigning behind every sip. *Tequila Made Me Do It* invites you to let go, relax, and enjoy a journey through Mexico, along the shimmering Pacific Acapulco Riviera, through the buzzing rush of Mexico City streets, all the way to a sea of blue agave fields in the highlands of Jalisco. With a Margarita in one hand and this book in the other, take a sip, sit back, and enjoy the ride.

A BRIEF HISTORY OF AGAVE

THE LEGEND OF MAYAHUEL

Mayahuel was the goddess of *maguey*, the agave plant family, within the Nahuatl creation story. Legend says that she was one of the *tzitzimime*, or spirits, that lived as stars in the sky, alongside her grandmother Tzitzimitl (Celestial Demon of Darkness that blocks the sun from shining). It was said that when Earth was created and the gods gave men all the crops and sustenance they needed, they realized that it was simply not enough. Something was missing that would create joy in their hearts and spark their passions.

It was then that Quetzalcoatl (God of the Wind and Feathered Serpent) searched the heavens for Mayahuel, to return her to Earth to find a solution for making men happy. After escaping from her guardian grandmother, the goddess Mayahuel and Quetzalcoatl fell in love on their way back to Earth. When her grandmother realized that Mayahuel was gone, she and the other *tzitzimime* chased Mayahuel. As soon as they reached Earth, the couple attempted to hide, transforming themselves into a tree with two single branches. The *tzitzimime*

7

destroyed the branch of Mayahuel, shredding her to pieces and leaving the branch of Quetzalcoatl intact. The inconsolable god picked up the pieces of his beloved and buried them in a nearby field. From her remains, a beautiful plant with large, pointed leaves eventually emerged. This is the *maguey*, from which, when its trunk is scraped, a sweet liquid flows. When fermented, that liquid becomes octli, or pulque.

That was how, tragically, the mission was accomplished. The two gods managed to awaken the joy in men, but at great personal cost. Represented as a young woman with multiple breasts from which the aguamiel, or honey water, flows, Mayahuel feeds the Centzon Totochtin, or 400 Rabbits, gods of drunkenness and pulque. The cult to Mayahuel has come to be associated with fertility, Earth, and the plant world.

A NOBLE PLANT
Agave (n.) From Greek *agauos* "noble, illustrious"

It is no coincidence that the taxonomical name for this genus of plants stems from the Greek word for nobility. In Mexico, referred to locally as *maguey*, agave plants are scattered throughout the landscape, from the northwestern state of Sonora all the way down to the southeastern Yucatan Peninsula. Food, drink, medicine, fuel, fibers, fertilizer, and the construction of homes are just some of the things this plant was used for by the early settlers of Mesoamerica, and the use of agave in cooking and fibers persists in Mexico to this day.

As a key part of the survival and establishment of these tribes, Mexico became the center for domestication and diversification of agave plants. Varietals were selected for their fibers, their aguamiel (honey water), or for the high sugar content provided after the hearts were cooked. As a result, agaves have their highest concentration of varietals in Mexico. Of the more than 200 species of agaves known to

exist in the Americas, more than 150 of them are found in Mexico, and 129—or 69 percent—are exclusive to Mexico. This makes them one of the most conspicuous symbols of the Mexican territory. Found mostly in arid and semi-arid regions of Mexico, agaves can be seen in more than 75 percent of the country's landscape and have the capacity to adapt to the most unfavorable conditions, including long periods of drought and high temperatures.

One of the most remarkable aspects of agaves is their age. The larger species can reach their maturity between 10 and 25 years, while smaller species can grow up to four and five years. This often overlooked characteristic of agaves is what makes tequila and mezcal production so unique and rare. While other neutral spirits acquire flavor and character from being aged for years in wooden barrels, agave spirits acquire these characteristics from years of the plants remaining in the fields, absorbing properties from the soil and energy from the moon and sun, giving rise to the term *reposado en campo,* or aged in fields.

FROM MEXICO WITH LOVE
Protected designations of origin
A designation of origin is used to recognize products that have originated from a specific region, whose quality and characteristics are derived from the environment in which they were developed. Mexico proudly boasts 14 protected designations of origin, which include spirits such as tequila, mezcal, bacanora, sotol, and charanda.

These designations preserve the tradition and production processes that make each product unique, and they also protect the integrity and quality by making it impossible to be replicated outside of their designated regions. Protected designations of origin exist all over the world. In Mexico, they are governed by the Law of Industrial Property, but some of the PDOs are also recognized and protected worldwide by the Lisbon Agreement, of which Mexico has been a member since 1958. The first Mexican PDO recognized by the Lisbon Agreement, and one of the most emblematic, was tequila in the year 1974.

TEQUILA

Tequila: The universal word for Mexico. Say "Mexico" anywhere in the world, and the immediate response is almost certain to be: "TEQUILA!" Tequila, as the title of this book suggests, has made us dance till the break of dawn, given us the courage to finally go up to that person at the bar, or simply let go of the worries of the world. Recognized worldwide as Mexico's national drink, tequila is synonymous with celebration, Mexican pride, and romance. But what exactly is tequila, and why can't we get enough of it?

The original term for the spirit now known as tequila was Vino de Mezcal de Tequila. Long before the declaration of any PDO, the New Spain recognized any agave spirit as a Vino de Mezcal; "de Tequila" referred to its region. In this case, the village of Jalisco has become known as the birthplace of this popular spirit. It wasn't until 1887 that the term Vino de Mezcal was dropped, and "tequila" was recognized around the world.

Tequila is the product made from the fermentation and distillation of cooked agave juices. In this case, the Agave tequilana Weber—a blue agave varietal that grows in arid and semi-arid regions of Mexico. As one of Mexico's most recognizable PDOs, it can only be produced within the states of Jalisco, Guanajuato, Nayarit, Michoacan, and Tamaulipas over nearly 48,560 hectares (120,000 acres). Each plant takes eight to ten years to mature to be harvested. Enter the *jimador,* who skillfully slashes all the leaves from the agave, leaving only the *piña*, or heart.

Today's production process is essentially the same as in the 15th century, with a few technological advances. The agaves were cut into two to four pieces and placed in an extensive stone-lined hole/oven in the ground, with wood at the bottom. The oven remained covered with dirt until the agaves were fully roasted, a process that could take 24 to 72 hours. Once cooked, the juices were extracted in a *tahona*: A circular track where a large round stone would turn several times over the agaves, pulled by a mule, crushing and separating the sweet juice and fibers, or must. The juices were then carried by buckets into fermenting tanks (often made of wood, clay, or leather hide). The musts were agitated and left to ferment naturally (using wild yeasts) over the course of 12 to 18 days.

Once fermentation was completed, the liquid was placed in copper pots or alembic stills. The fermented liquid was boiled to separate water from the alcohol through evaporation, to be condensed in an iron cauldron with cold water. The alcohol was again distilled to reach the desired proof and to separate the heads and tail—undesirable byproducts of distillation. The alcohol obtained in the middle of the process was the desired quality, known as the tequila real.

Changes to production have been minimal. Instead of underground ovens, brick ovens or steel autoclaves are used. The use of mechanical crushers has also reduced time and increased juice extraction. Including non-agave sugars and controlled yeasts has accelerated fermentation. Stainless steel has replaced traditional wooden tanks, and steel stills for copper pot stills.

THE RISE OF TEQUILA

After the 7th-century invasion of the Iberian Peninsula by Muslim forces, distillation knowledge was adopted by the Spaniards, who brought it to the New World. There, they encountered an indigenous population that enjoyed the inebriating effect of sweet fermented agave juice. Once the conquerors ran out of their high-proof brandy, they shared their distillation techniques with local tribes, to transform the local fermented drink into a spirit known as mexicali (meaning "cooked agave").

While initially tequila was produced for consumption only, the *hacendados* could see commercial potential. It wasn't long before the popularity of Vino de Mezcal began to pose an economic threat to Spanish alcohol, and authorities of New Spain banned agave spirits. In 1785, the first formal prohibition took place, in the form of a Royal

Order. This led to clandestine production and an underground market. However, controlling the distilleries became a costly task, and in 1795 the Spanish king gave consent to Juan Antonio Cuervo to produce tequila.

Over the years, Mexico rode out tumultuous times, and tequila's popularity reflected the contemporary situation. The Europeanization of Mexico in the late 19th century once again favored European spirits, diminishing the tequila industry. However, years after the Mexican Revolution, local and global affairs led to the resurgence of tequila.

The prohibition of alcohol in the United States from 1920 to 1933 opened the gates for tequila to enter American hearts, crossing the Bravo River illegally and satisfying thirsty palates in speakeasies across the country. Back in Mexico, the Golden Age of Mexican cinema in the 1930s gave rise to the stereotype of the Mexican man—a tequila-drinking, cattle-ranching, mariachi-singing womanizer—and tequila was once again a national symbol.

TYPES OF TEQUILA
The rise of tequila's popularity and its distinct flavor allowed opportunists outside of Mexico to try and cash in on tequila's success by mimicking spirits and trying to pass them off as original tequilas. In 1973, some of the main *Tequileros* began lobbying for the declaration of a protected designation of origin, to cover the states of Jalisco and Nayarit. On November 22, 1974, with the addition of the states of Tamaulipas, Michoacan, and Guanajuato, the Ministry of Industry and Commerce declared the Protected Designation of Origin "Tequila."

TEQUILA BREAKDOWN
Tequila is classified into two categories depending on the quantity of agave

sugars and other sugars added during fermentation. After the tequila is distilled, it is sold in four main presentations, depending on the amount of time aged in oak barrels.

100% Agave—As the classification suggests, this is the spirit obtained from only the sugars of Agave tequilana Weber or blue agave, cultivated in the territory included in the Declaration of the PDO.

Mixto—Spirit obtained from musts that have been enriched or mixed with sugars other than Agave tequilana Weber, in a percentage no greater than 49%.

Blanco/Plata (Silver)—Unaged tequila.

Joven/Oro (Gold)—A blend of blanco tequila with reposado, añejo, or extra añejo.

Reposado—Tequila aged in oak barrels for less than two months. A blend between reposado and añejo or extra añejo tequilas can also be considered reposado.

Añejo—Tequila aged in oak barrels for a minimum of one year. A blend of añejo and extra añejo tequilas.

Extra Añejo—Tequila aged in oak barrels for a minimum of three years.

MEZCAL

Para todo mal mezcal, para todo bien tambien.
"For everything bad, mezcal, for everything good as well."

Mezcal is the second-most popular Protected Designation of Origin of Mexico's spirits. Unlike tequila's standardized production method, mezcal is all about diversity. It can be made from over 40 agave varietals found in the nine designated states. Oaxaca, Guerrero, Guanajuato, San Luis Potosí, Zacatecas, Durango, Tamaulipas, Michoacán, and Puebla are all part of the mezcal PDO, spanning 193,000 sq. mi. and making it the largest PDO in the world. But this enigmatic spirit hasn't always been popular. Long ostracized, mezcal was portrayed as the poor man's spirit. It is no secret that tequila has played a role in tarnishing mezcal's reputation, favoring tequila over other agave spirits.

But even as discerning palates indulged in tequila, there were always those whose own defying nature, in the quest for adventure, would wander into strange territories, much like Alice, and tumble down the rabbit hole of mezcal. Aficionados would render themselves enamored of the fiery spirit of Oaxaca. Mezcal may have been neglected over the years, but to anyone with a desire for the unknown, it remains a spirit with the power to inspire imbibers for generations to come.

The production process for mezcal is the same as tequila. However, the vast majority of mezcals produced today still possess an artisanal quality of the elements and processes used during roasting, crushing, fermentation, and distillation. In Oaxaca, where more than 80 percent of mezcals are produced, a traditional *palenque* (distillery) is composed of an underground, stone-lined oven, a *tahona,* wooden open-air fermentation tanks and simple copper pot stills. These parts, especially the signature cooking method of roasting the agaves in an underground firewood oven, is what gives mezcal its distinct smokiness. The production capacity of mezcal is much smaller than tequila. The production of a single *palenque* with two 92-gallon (350-liter) stills can range from 2,640–3,170 gallons (10,000–12,000 liters) a year. In other words, mezcal is micro-distilled.

The most common agave varietal used in mezcal is Agave espadín (*angustifolia Haw*), whose cultivation originated in Oaxaca in the mid-20th century. Today, more than 75 percent of mezcal is from espadín agaves, chosen for their larger *piñas* and higher sugar concentration. Wild agaves are also used to create exclusive variations, elevating them to the luxury spirits market. Agaves like the Potatorum or Tobala can be found in isolated regions in the high sierras of Oaxaca. These smaller agaves are highly aromatic and can be complex in flavor, with notes of lavender, cardamom, and lime zest. Another popular wild agave is the

Madrecuixe, with earthy notes of cacao, clay, and butterscotch.

The rise in mezcal's popularity has not only generated income to some of Mexico's most isolated regions, it has also allowed migrant laborers to return to their communities and work in their forgotten trade. The increase in demand for rare agave spirits has generated opportunities for rural populations to create long-term businesses and the promise of a future for generations to come.

TYPES OF MEZCAL
The PDO for mezcal was declared in 1994. Mezcal is predominantly produced with 100% Agave and can be classified into the following categories:

Mezcal (Industrial)—Mezcal produced using modern technology that can include autoclaves, mechanical crushers, stainless steel fermentation tanks, and continuous or column stills.
Mezcal Artisanal—Mezcal produced using traditional methods, including underground stone-lined ovens, *tahonas*, or manual crushing, fermentation tanks made from wood, clay, stone, or hide, and traditional copper alembic stills.
Mezcal Ancestral—Mezcal produced using the same methods as the Mezcal Artisanal, with the added use of clay vessels for distillation.

MEZCAL DE PECHUGA—Mezcal distilled with additional ingredients can also be known as Mezcal de Pechuga. This is triple-distilled in single pot copper stills with a maceration of seasonal fruits and spices, including *tejocote*, guava, pineapple, apples, cinnamon, and clove, depending on the producer. After a batch of espadín mezcal is made, it is added back to the still with the fruit. A raw turkey breast is suspended over the still in a mesh cloth. The mezcal distills again, absorbing oils from the fruit. While it evaporates, it permeates the turkey breast, obtaining fats and oils from the meat's juices, adding a velvety texture to the resulting spirit.

MARGARITA

POPPING UP LIKE DAISIES

She turns 70 this year, and like many popular cocktails, the history of the Margarita is as mysterious as it is filled with holes. No one seems quite able to pinpoint the origin of this beloved cocktail, most likely because every time someone tries to tell the story, they're usually on their fourth or fifth. Given the multiple fan theories for how it originated, where the name came from, and who the first Margarita was made for, digging up the history of this cocktail is like trying to figure out who really shot JFK.

One such story begins in a bar in Ensenada, frequented by Margarita Henkel, the daughter of a German ambassador. Some believe it was named after starlet Margarita Cansino (aka Rita Hayworth), who would often perform at the Agua Caliente Race Track, where bartender Danny Negrete claimed to have invented it. However, after falling down the rabbit hole of cocktail conspiracies, it seems safe to assume that the source for what is considered one of the original ingredients, *la famille* Cointreau, is truly in the know. Despite the controversy, the most accepted version, according to Alfred Cointreau, took place in a grand, lush setting on the Mexican Pacific Riviera.

The time was the end of the 1940s, and the scene was Acapulco jet-set glamour. Late-night parties and celebrations glittered this jewel of the Pacific with young Hollywood starlets. As a product of its time, the lovely Margarita, highly coveted by the American palate for its balanced sweet and savory flavor, was first concocted by a Dallas-native socialite by the name of Margaret Sames in a posh Acapulco villa. Margaret claims to have created the drink for a gathering of her closest friends while vacationing in Acapulco in 1948, using two of her favorite spirits: Tequila and Cointreau. Among them would be Tommy Hilton, who then put it on the cocktail bar menu of the Hilton hotel chain, and the rest is history.

16

SYRUPS & TEAS

SIMPLE SYRUP

Pour equal parts water and sugar into a pan. Heat until the ingredients have dissolved, then simmer and stir until completely clear. Leave to cool. Store in an airtight container in the refrigerator for up to 3–4 weeks.

AGUA FRESCA

2 cups dried hibiscus flowers (or use jarred hibiscus flowers)
¾ cup granulated sugar

Bring 50 fluid ounces of water to a boil in a pan and add the flowers and sugar. Stir continuously for 1 minute. Remove from the heat and leave to cool. Strain the mixture through a sieve, while pressing on the flowers to extract all the liquid. Store in an airtight container in the refrigerator for up to 10 days.

ROSE WATER

petals from 2 roses
1 teaspoon tequila

Combine 16 fluid ounces of water, the rose petals, and tequila in a pan and simmer until the petals are pale. Strain into a sealed container. Keep refrigerated and store for up to 1 week.

CHAMOMILE SYRUP

1 cup unrefined sugar
4 tablespoons loose-leaf chamomile tea (or 4 chamomile tea bags)

Combine 8 fluid ounces of water and the sugar in a pan and simmer, stirring constantly until the sugar dissolves. Steep the tea in 12 fluid ounces of the syrup for 20 minutes while it is still hot. Strain, allow to cool, and keep refrigerated for 1–2 weeks.

CINNAMON SYRUP/CINNAMON GRAPEFRUIT SYRUP

2 cups refined sugar
1 teaspoon ground cinnamon
juice of 2–3 whole grapefruits, peel reserved (if using)

Combine 8 fluid ounces of water with sugar in a pan and bring to a boil. Turn off the heat and stir until the sugar completely dissolves. Add the cinnamon (and the grapefruit peels, if using) and leave to steep. Cool to room temperature (approximately 20 minutes), then strain out the grapefruit peels, if using. For the Cinnamon Grapefruit Syrup only, add 8 fluid ounces of the grapefruit juice to the syrup. Stir and refrigerate. Keep in an airtight container in the refrigerator for up to 2 weeks.

CITRUS CORDIAL

juice and finely grated zest of
 2 oranges
juice and finely grated zest of
 1 lemon
3 cups caster sugar
½ tablespoon citric acid
16 fluid ounces boiling water

Begin this recipe 1 day ahead. Add all the ingredients to a pan over medium heat. Stir constantly until the sugar has dissolved, then remove from the heat and cover with a lid or plastic wrap. Leave at room temperature overnight. Strain and pour into a sterilized, airtight bottle, and keep refrigerated for up to 4 weeks. Use for cocktails, or just add ice and sparkling water for a refreshing drink.

HIBISCUS TEA

¼ cup dried hibiscus flowers

Bring the hibiscus flowers and 16 fluid ounces of water to a boil in a saucepan. Once the water begins to boil, remove from the heat, cover, and steep for 20 minutes. Strain the tea into your desired container and allow to cool. Seal in an airtight container and refrigerate for up to 1 week.

GINGER SYRUP

1 cup cane or granulated sugar
2 cups peeled and thinly sliced
 ginger

Combine 8 fluid ounces of water, the sugar, and ginger in a pan and simmer over medium-low heat. Stir thoroughly until the sugar has dissolved and continue to simmer for 30 minutes. Strain through a sieve and cool to room temperature. Store in an airtight container and keep refrigerated for 2-3 weeks.

HORCHATA

1 cup white rice (uncooked)
2-3 cinnamon sticks
1 14-ounce can
 condensed milk

1 12-ounce can
evaporated milk
1 tablespoon vanilla extract

Heat 16 fluid ounces of water in a pan until boiling. Remove from the heat and add the rice and cinnamon sticks. Soak the rice in the hot water for at least 1 hour. Remove the cinnamon sticks and mix the rice and soaking water in a blender until the rice is completely blended. Pour the mixture into a large jug and add the condensed milk, evaporated milk, and vanilla extract. Stir well. Ensure the liquid is cool before using. This can be kept in the refrigerator for up to 1 week.

HIBISCUS SYRUP

1 cup sugar
½ cup dried hibiscus flowers

Combine 8 fluid ounces of water and the sugar in a pan and bring to a boil, stirring continuously until the sugar has dissolved. Remove from the heat and add the hibiscus flowers. Leave for 15 minutes and strain. Refrigerate and keep in an airtight container for up to 2 weeks.

BLACKBERRY VINAIGRETTE

1 cup blackberries
2¾ fluid ounces red wine vinegar
3 tablespoons olive oil
1 tablespoon agave nectar (or substitute with maple syrup)
salt and freshly ground black pepper

Combine the blackberries and 2 fluid ounces of water in a food processor or blender and purée until an even consistency. Strain the puréed berries repeatedly through a sieve until the seeds are removed. Combine the purée with the vinegar, oil, and agave nectar and mix well. Taste and add some salt and pepper. Keep refrigerated in an airtight container for up to 3 weeks.

REGRET SHRUB

1 cup fresh turmeric root
4 whole oranges (with peel)
4 lemons (with peel)
1 whole pineapple, peeled
8 fluid ounces rice vinegar
8 fluid ounces Honey Syrup (see below)

Juice the turmeric root, oranges, lemons, and pineapple in a juice extractor. Add the vinegar and honey syrup and mix well. Store

honey syrup and mix well. Store in an airtight container in the refrigerator for up to 2 weeks.

TEPACHE

½ cup brown sugar
½ pineapple (with skin), washed and diced
2 whole cloves

Dissolve the brown sugar in 32 fluid ounces of water over medium heat in a pan. Once dissolved, allow to cool. To a large glass jar, add the pineapple, sugar-water, and cloves. Cover with a muslin cloth and leave to stand in a cool, dry place for 3 days. The tepache will become cloudy, forming a white foam on the top. Scoop out the white foam before using. Store in an airtight container in the refrigerator for 1 week.

JALAPEÑO SIMPLE SYRUP

1 cup cane or granulated sugar
1 jalapeño sliced lengthways (no seeds)

Combine 8 fluid ounces of water and the sugar in a pan and bring to a boil, stirring constantly to dissolve the sugar. Remove from the heat and add the sliced jalapeño. Cover and steep for 10 minutes. Strain the syrup carefully and allow to cool. Keep refrigerated in an airtight container for up to 1 week.

HONEY SYRUP

Place equal parts honey and water in a pan and boil. Reduce the heat to a simmer and stir until the honey has completely dissolved. Allow to cool and keep refrigerated in an airtight container for up to 4 weeks.

ORANGE AND SAFFRON SYRUP

2 cups cane or granulated sugar
1 ounce saffron
juice of 3–4 navel oranges, peel reserved

Combine 8 fluid ounces of water and the sugar in a pan and bring to a boil. Turn off the heat and stir the sugar until it completely dissolves. Add the saffron and the orange peel and leave to steep for 20 minutes while it cools. Once the syrup is at room temperature, strain out the saffron and orange peel. Add 8 fluid ounces of the orange juice to the syrup. Stir and keep refrigerated in an airtight container for up to 2 weeks.

THE RECIPES

21

MARGARITA

CLASSIC MARGARITA

(Makes 1)

Quite possibly named after a beautiful woman, the Margarita is believed to be the Mexican version of a traditional Daisy. The Daisy is a cocktail that combines a shot of liquor, lemon juice, and orange cordial. Regardless of how the Margarita came to be, its foolproof recipe and balanced flavor with sweet, savory, and tart notes has made it not only the quintessential tequila cocktail, but also one of the most popular cocktails in history.

Ingredients
1 fluid ounce freshly squeezed lime juice, plus extra for the rim
2 fluid ounces tequila (blanco or reposado)
1 fluid ounce Cointreau
salt, for the rim

Instructions
Moisten the rim of a double rocks glass with water or lime juice and, holding it upside down, dip the rim into a flat dish filled with table or kosher salt. Place the tequila, Cointreau, and lime juice in a cocktail shaker filled with ice. Shake and strain the drink into the prepared glass filled with ice cubes and serve.

FROZEN MARGARITA

(Makes 4)

At the height of tequila's popularity in the 1970s, the slushy, frozen version of the Margarita was popular all over the United States. It was in 1971 that a young Mexican-American with the dream of becoming a successful restaurateur was struggling to expedite an array of blended frozen Margaritas to his clientele. Then Mariano Martinez had a revelation. After a trip to the local 7-Eleven store, he saw a Slurpee frozen drinks machine and knew what he had to do. Unable to acquire such a machine, Martinez adapted an old soft-serve ice-cream machine to streamline the production of what has become one of the world's favorite frozen alcoholic beverages. To this day, Martinez's iconic invention sits at the Smithsonian's National Museum of American History.

Ingredients

8 fluid ounces freshly squeezed lime juice, plus extra for the rim
8 fluid ounces blanco tequila
4 fluid ounces triple sec (preferably Cointreau)
4 cups of ice
salt, for the rim (optional)
lime wheels or wedges, to garnish

Instructions

Moisten the rim of a classic margarita glass with water or lime juice and, holding it upside down, dip the rim into a flat dish filled with table or kosher salt, if using. Place all the remaining ingredients, except the garnish, in a blender. Blend until slushy throughout and add more ice if necessary (if the consistency is more liquid than slush). Pour the drink into the prepared glass and garnish with lime wheels or wedges.

TOMMY'S MARGARITA

(Makes 1)

Before Bethenny Frankel convinced women that tequila was a girl's best friend, the Skinny Margarita was already a thing at Julio Bermejo's Tommy's Mexican Restaurant in San Francisco, California. Created in the early 1990s, Bermejo played around with the Margarita and swapped the original orange liqueur for the more natural sweet flavor of agave nectar, influencing the future natural and seasonal ingredients movement in cocktails. But while agave nectar may seem like a healthier alternative to sugar, its often overlooked high fructose content is something that should be taken into consideration. As with all things in life, balance is key.

Ingredients
1 fluid ounce freshly squeezed lime juice, plus extra for the rim
2 fluid ounces 100% agave blanco tequila
½ fluid ounce agave nectar
salt, for the rim

Instructions
Moisten the rim of a double rocks glass with water or lime juice and, holding it upside down, dip the rim into a flat dish filled with table or kosher salt. Place the tequila, agave nectar, and lime juice in a cocktail shaker filled with ice. Shake and strain the drink into the prepared glass filled with ice cubes and serve.

CADILLAC MARGARITA

(Makes 1)

A Cadillac Margarita is exactly what it sounds like: A grandiose, upscale version of the original. More is more in this cocktail, but the recipe remains simple. Instead of using tequila blanco, upgrade to an aged top-shelf reposado or añejo tequila. Skimping on this Margarita is totally off limits. It only deserves the best of the best. Swapping the traditional white orange liqueurs, like Cointreau and triple sec, for the cognac-based Grand Marnier makes this Margarita the belle of the ball.

Ingredients

¾ fluid ounce freshly squeezed lime juice, plus extra for the rim
1 ½ fluid ounces premium reposado or añejo tequila
1 fluid ounce Grand Marnier
salt, for the rim (optional)

Instructions

Moisten the rim of a double rocks glass with water or lime juice and, holding it upside down, dip the rim into a flat dish filled with table or kosher salt, if using. Place the tequila, Grand Marnier, and lime juice in a cocktail shaker filled with ice. Shake and strain the drink into the glass filled with ice cubes and serve.

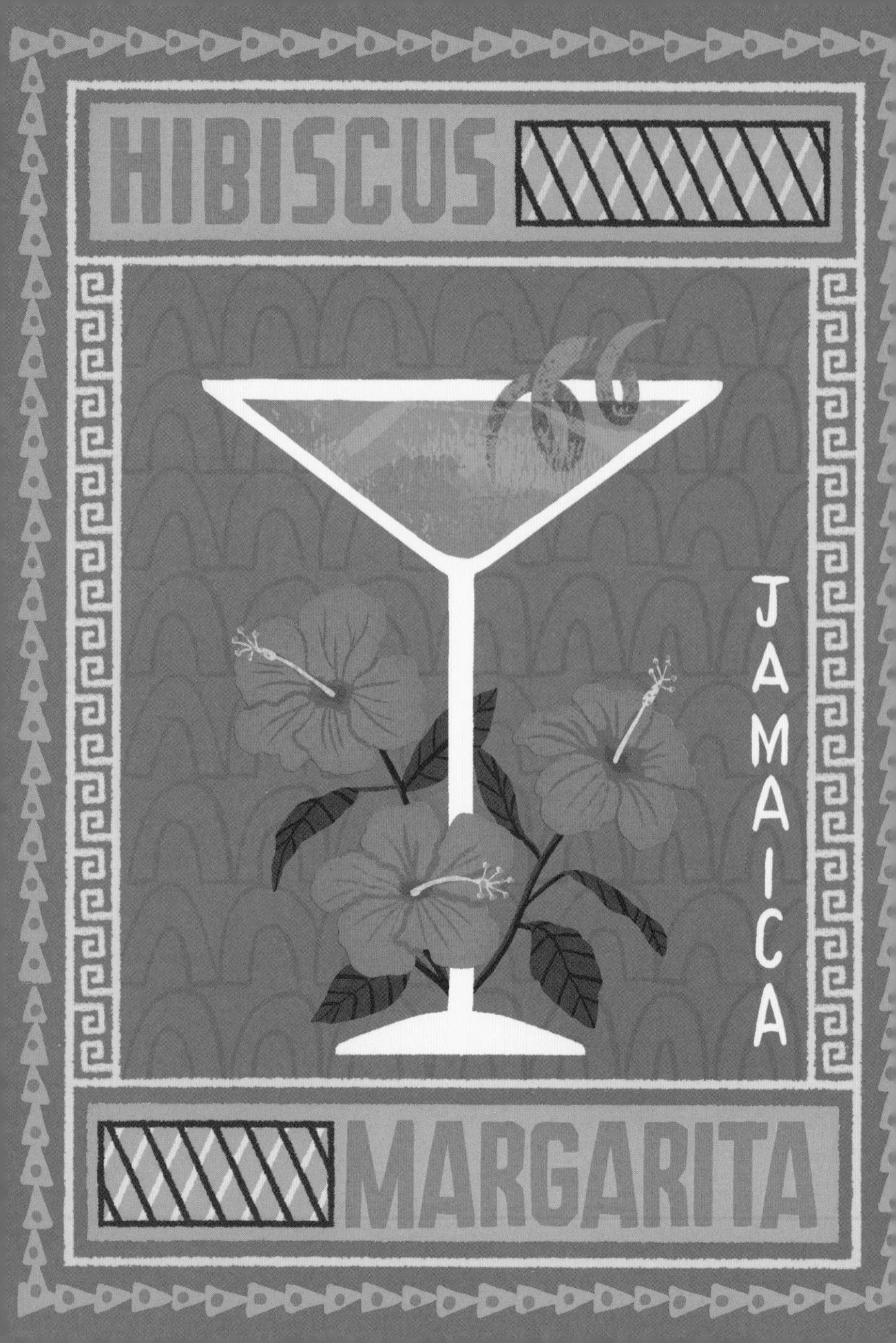
HIBISCUS
JAMAICA
MARGARITA

HIBISCUS MARGARITA

(Makes 1)

This cocktail takes on a bold approach, as the traditional Margarita dresses in red for a vibrant Jamaican variation. With a deep scarlet color, and simultaneous sweet and tangy flavor, the Jamaican flower, or *Hibiscus sabdariffa*, came to Mexico aboard Manila Galleons (Spanish trading ships), which traipsed across the Pacific Ocean as early as 1565, linking the Philippines with Mexico. The first port to find this exotic flower in Mexico was Acapulco. It quickly became a staple of Mexican cuisine and, of course, its aguas frescas. In this Margarita, the tart and floral quality of the hibiscus flower enhances the bouquet of notes found in a well-made blanco tequila.

Ingredients
3 fluid ounces Agua Fresca (page 17)
1 ½ fluid ounces blanco tequila
1 fluid ounce Simple Syrup (page 17)
½ fluid ounce freshly squeezed lime juice

Instructions
First, prepare a margarita glass by chilling it in the freezer, or filling it with ice cubes and allowing it to stand (before tossing out the ice cubes prior to pouring in the drink). Place all the ingredients in a cocktail shaker filled with ice and shake well. Strain into the chilled glass.

TAMARIND MARGARITA

(Makes 1)

Tamarind has been a delicacy in Mexico for generations, but like many things in this culturally rich location, its origins lay in a very distant place. The history of the culinary use of tamarind is closely linked to India, where it was introduced by the Arabs so long ago that few Indians realize it actually originated in Africa. For centuries it has been used in the production of different kinds of foods and beverages. The Spaniards were responsible for bringing tamarind to the Americas, where its cultivation quickly spread along the Pacific and other tropical areas. It has long since been part of the traditional cuisine of this area, especially in places like Acapulco, where sugar and chili have been added to create one of the most popular Mexican sweets. Besides sweets, tamarind can be found in sweet-and-sour sauces alongside beef or fish, and in beverages, often accompanying tequila.

Ingredients

¼ fluid ounce freshly squeezed lime juice, plus extra for the rim
2 fluid ounces blanco tequila
¾ fluid ounce tamarind paste
¾ fluid ounce Simple Syrup (page 17)
Tajin seasoning with lime, or chili powder, for the rim

Instructions

Moisten the rim of a double rocks glass with water or lime juice and, holding it upside down, dip the rim into a flat dish filled with Tajin seasoning or chili powder. Place the remaining ingredients in a cocktail shaker filled with ice. Shake and strain the drink into the prepared glass filled with ice cubes and serve.

INFANTE

(Makes 1)

Pedro Infante was a humble man who, thanks to his charisma and talent, quickly became a Mexican idol. Having appeared in over 50 films in his short life (he died at the age of 39), Infante is remembered as a charming ladies' man who today remains one of Mexico's most revered cultural icons and whose songs captivated and influenced entire generations during and after the Golden Age of Mexican cinema in the 1940s and '50s. As a tribute to this enchanting Mexican idol, the Infante is a cocktail that allures to the palate with a hint of sensuality granted by the orgeat (almond) syrup and a spray of rose water.

Ingredients
2 fluid ounces blanco tequila
¾ fluid ounce freshly squeezed lime juice
¾ fluid ounce orgeat syrup (such as Torani)
a spray of rose water (home-made, page 17; or store-bought) and a dusting of grated nutmeg, to garnish

Instructions
Place all the ingredients, except the garnish, in a shaker filled with ice and shake well. Fine strain into a double rocks glass filled with ice cubes. Spray a little rose water and sprinkle a little grated nutmeg on top to serve.

MEZCALITA

(Makes 1)

When it comes to the incredible range of Margarita variations, there is one version that simply cannot go unnoticed. It is also the simplest. The Mezcalita, or Mezcal Margarita, tastes exactly as it sounds—a smokier, more rugged version of the popular classic. Made with mezcal instead of tequila, the sweet citric notes of the espadín mezcal complement the delicious caramel agave notes of the agave nectar, creating an earthier and bolder flavor profile. Taming the smokiness with a bit of lime, the Mezcalita is the perfect way to introduce mezcal to any novices, who haven't yet decided to make the mezcal leap. Don't forget to add a bit of fiery sal de gusano, made with crushed agave worms, to the rim of the glass for extra kick.

Ingredients

1 fluid ounce freshly squeezed lime juice, plus extra for the rim
2 fluid ounces espadín mezcal
1 fluid ounce agave nectar
sal de gusano (see Note below) or regular salt, for the rim

Instructions

Moisten the rim of a martini glass with water or lime juice and, holding it upside down, dip the rim into a flat dish filled with the sal de gusano. Place all the remaining ingredients in a cocktail shaker filled with ice and shake well. Fine strain into the prepared glass and serve.

Note: Vegans and vegetarians be warned. Sal de gusano is made of crushed agave worms, chili, and salt.

BESO MANZANILLA
(Makes 1)

This cocktail is as refreshing as it is comforting. The delicate flowers of the chamomile plant are most commonly known for their health benefits, including stress-reduction and as a cure for muscle spasms. Chamomile can also help with anxiety and depression and is an anti-inflammatory and insomnia cure. The floral and honeyed elements in the chamomile syrup blend perfectly with the smoky, vegetal aspect of the mezcal, to create the perfect sophisticated cocktail, bringing nothing but feel-good vibes as you sip it.

Ingredients
¾ fluid ounce Cointreau
¾ fluid ounce mezcal
¾ fluid ounce blanco tequila
¾ fluid ounce freshly squeezed lemon juice
2 bar spoons of Chamomile Syrup (page 17)
a sprig of fresh chamomile, to garnish

Instructions
Place all the ingredients, except the garnish, in a cocktail shaker filled with ice and shake well. Strain into a double rocks glass filled with a large block of ice. Garnish with the sprig of fresh chamomile.

SMOKY CHILI MARGARITA

(Makes 1)

Whether they're fresh or dried, large or small, pickled, sweet or smoky, chilis can be found in almost any Mexican dish—even in the drinks! If you're into heat, then this is the Margarita for you. This simple, mezcal-based Margarita will allow you to appreciate mezcal's intricate character but in a familiar setting. You may think that this version is for the more adventurous palate, but by adding a bit of spice to the mix, the mezcal's smokiness emerges beautifully while balancing with the cooling effect of the lime.

Ingredients
¼ teaspoon chipotle in adobo sauce
1 ½ fluid ounces espadín mezcal
1 fluid ounce agave nectar
¾ fluid ounce freshly squeezed lime juice
a lime wheel, to garnish

Instructions
Place all the ingredients, except the garnish, in a cocktail shaker filled with ice and shake well. Strain into a martini or double rocks glass over ice. Garnish with a lime wheel to serve.

MARGARITA COLADA

(Makes 1)

If you like piña coladas like the 1979 pop song by Rupert Holmes, you'll definitely love this tropical Margarita. And if you love getting caught in the rain, just like the famous song suggests, the Margarita Colada will be everything you need to get out of the same old dull routine. Bring a little paradise to your Margarita with the tropical flavors of pineapple and coconut, which pair perfectly with the earthy and vegetal flavors of tequila. Perhaps you'll even find the love of your life while sipping away on this exotic getaway.

Ingredients
2 fluid ounces tequila
2 fluid ounces pineapple juice
1 fluid ounce coconut milk
½ fluid ounce freshly squeezed lime juice
1–2 teaspoons agave nectar
desiccated or shredded coconut and a
   pineapple wedge, to garnish

Instructions
Place the tequila, pineapple juice, coconut milk, lime juice, and agave nectar in a cocktail shaker filled with ice. Shake and strain into a double rocks glass over ice. Garnish with the coconut and a pineapple wedge.

BITTER ORANGE MARGARITA

(Makes 1)

With the resurgence of classic cocktails came the resurgence of bitters. But what are bitters exactly? Originally made for medicinal purposes, bitters are the infusion of a neutral spirit with spices, roots, fruits, seeds, etc. They are concentrated in flavor and are typically sold in small bottles for use in classic stirred cocktails, traditionally using only a dash or two. However, in this rich version of the Margarita, the Angostura bitters get to share the stage with the nutty, butterscotch notes found in the oak-aged tequila. An egg white is added for texture and richness, which, alongside the citrus of the lemon juice, creates a magnificent combination and silky texture.

Ingredients
1 fluid ounce añejo tequila
1 fluid ounce Angostura orange bitters
1 fluid ounce freshly squeezed lemon juice
1 egg white
orange twist, to garnish

Instructions
Add the tequila, bitters, lemon juice, and egg white to a cocktail shaker. Dry shake (without ice) for 20 seconds, then add ½ cup of ice and shake again. Double strain into a coupe glass and garnish with an orange twist to serve.

STRAWBERRY MARGARITA SPRITZ

(Makes 1)

By now you've probably realized that there are infinite variations to what a Margarita can become. Three basic ingredients will define her: agave, a sweet liqueur, and tart citrus. But what happens when you add a touch of Champagne to instantly elevate the occasion? The result is a sweet and fizzy Margarita that will make any given moment feel like Sunday brunch.

Ingredients
1 fluid ounce freshly squeezed lime juice, plus extra for the rim
1½ fluid ounces blanco tequila
1 fluid ounce fresh strawberry purée
1 teaspoon agave nectar
Champagne, to top up
salt, for the rim

Instructions
Moisten the rim of a coupe glass with water or lime juice. Holding the glass upside down, dip the rim into a flat dish filled with table or kosher salt. Place all the remaining ingredients, except the Champagne, in a cocktail shaker filled with ice and shake well. Strain into the prepared glass and top up with Champagne to serve.

SANGRITA CLASSIC

(Makes 4)

Named for its intense blood-red color, the Sangrita has been tequila's consort for over 70 years. Born in the cradle of the Tequila region, at a restaurant in Chapala, Jalisco, the first Sangrita was a simple mixture of orange juice, salt, and chili. It was created to chase and tame the strong crudeness of the house-made tequila at Don Mundo's and Doña Guadalupe Sanchez's famous 1920s restaurant (the name of which has been lost to time). Over the years, Sangrita recipes have evolved and taken on a life of their own, each variation becoming a representative of the region where it is made. Today's classic recipes include tomato juice and are recognized as staples of tequila-sipping culture.

Ingredients
8 fluid ounces tomato juice
4 fluid ounces freshly squeezed orange juice
¾ fluid ounce freshly squeezed lime juice
1 tablespoon Worcestershire sauce
½ tablespoon Tabasco sauce
1 tablespoon finely chopped onion
salt, to taste

Instructions
Mix all the ingredients in a blender and chill before serving. Serve in a shot glass next to a shot of tequila.

SANGRITA SWEET

(Makes 4)

This sweet Sangrita variation is ideal for mezcal. Besides being the perfect chaser, the Sangrita is meant to enhance the notes of the mezcal or tequila being sipped alongside it. The smokiness and bitter citrus notes of most espadín mezcals marry perfectly with the fresh, fruity sweetness of the pomegranate juice. The pairing makes each sip a more flavorful experience, highlighting the complexity and sophistication of the agave. But as each mezcal is known to have a personality of its own, Sangritas are intended to be playful, and the possibilities and flavor combinations are endless. Try swapping the pomegranate for grapefruit or pineapple juice and see which one pairs better with your preferred mezcal.

Ingredients

8 fluid ounces freshly squeezed orange juice
4 fluid ounces fresh, or from concentrate, pomegranate juice
2 fluid ounces freshly squeezed lime juice
1 teaspoon red chili powder
1 teaspoon cayenne pepper
salt, to taste

Instructions

Mix all the ingredients in a large jug and chill before serving. Serve in a shot glass next to a shot of mezcal or tequila.

TEQUILA NEGRONI

(Makes 1)

Originally a more intense version of the American cocktail, the Negroni's origins can be traced back to 1919, when Count Camillo Negroni, infatuated with stronger spirits, requested a bit of a kick be added to this classic libation. For nearly a century, gin, Campari, and vermouth have remained the go-to ingredients for the classic Negroni in Italian restaurants and bars the world over. With the resurgence of cocktail classics over the last decade, the Negroni has become a fundamental part of any cocktail menu and its basic components have led to the innovation and tweaking of the classic recipe. In this Mexican version of the Count's classic, simplicity is key.

Ingredients
1 fluid ounce Campari
1 fluid ounce blanco tequila
1 fluid ounce sweet vermouth
an orange twist, to garnish

Instructions
Fill a chilled double rocks glass with ice cubes.
Add the Campari, tequila, and vermouth. Stir well.
Garnish with a twist of orange peel to serve.

ANCHO NEGRONI

(Makes 1)

In my experience, any situation can be improved just by adding mezcal. This variation of the Negroni not only adds a bit of smoke to the mix, it also swaps the vermouth for Ancho Reyes, a unique Mexican liqueur based on a historic Pueblan recipe from 1927, adding a little extra spiciness to your life. The ancho chili flavors of the liqueur, combined with the smokiness of the mezcal, pepper this classic Italian cocktail with a dash of excitement and Mexican history.

Ingredients

1 fluid ounce Montelobos mezcal
1 fluid ounce Ancho Reyes chili liqueur
1 fluid ounce Campari
an orange slice, to garnish

Instructions

First, prepare a double rocks glass by chilling it in the freezer or filling it with ice (and tossing the ice cubes and replacing with fresh ones before pouring in the drink). Combine all the ingredients in a mixing glass with ice. Stir vigorously, strain with a cocktail sieve, and serve over ice in the chilled glass. Garnish with an orange slice to serve.

PALOMA CLASSIC

(Makes 1)

The history of the refreshing and tasty Paloma, possibly the most popular tequila cocktail in Mexico, can be traced back to one of the oldest bars in the country, situated in the small town of Tequila that gave its name to this fiery spirit. If you haven't yet heard of La Capilla, just a sip of this drink and you may find yourself booking the first flight there! Picture a small, humble cantina on the corner of a cobbled street, where celebrities, rock stars, and tequila aficionados flock from all corners of the world to try Don Javier Delgado Corona's cocktails, which include the classic Paloma, as well as a Coca-Cola, tequila, and lime highball known as the Batanga. If you're lucky enough, the iconic Don Javier (now in his 90s) might even serve you himself. This delicious mixture of bitter grapefruit juice with lime, salt, and tequila will awaken your senses and leave you asking for more.

Ingredients
2 fluid ounces blanco tequila
1 fluid ounce freshly squeezed grapefruit juice
½ fluid ounce freshly squeezed lime juice
a pinch of salt
1 tablespoon agave nectar
soda water, to top up
a grapefruit wedge or lime wedge, to garnish

Instructions
Mix all the ingredients, except the soda water and garnish, in a cocktail shaker filled with ice and shake for 15 seconds. Fill a collins glass with fresh ice cubes and strain the drink into the glass. Top up with soda water and stir briefly. Garnish with a grapefruit or lime wedge to serve.

PALOMA
CHULA VISTA
DE ABAJO
BAR
La Cappilla
CENTRO
RANCHITO
COLINAS
DEL
ROSARIO
LA MEZCALERA
TEXCALAME
TEQUILA
MEXICO

COCONUT PALOMA

(Makes 1)

If a trip to the Tequila region of Mexico is not exotic enough for you, imagine yourself on a Caribbean island retreat, sipping this beachy riff of the classic Paloma cocktail. The coconut not only adds a tropical element to this tasty classic, but the hydrating effects of the coconut water mixed with the high levels of vitamin C and the antioxidant properties of the grapefruit juice create a balance with the tequila to make this the perfect drink to enjoy on a hot summer day. And perhaps you can even convince yourself the vitamin C and coconut water make this a healthy drink!

Ingredients

2 fluid ounces reposado tequila
2 fluid ounces freshly squeezed grapefruit juice
2 fluid ounces coconut water
2 fluid ounces fresh grapefruit juice
2 fluid ounces soda water
a grapefruit wedge, to garnish

Instructions

Place all the ingredients, except the soda water and garnish, in a cocktail shaker filled with ice and shake for 15 seconds. Fill a collins or double rocks glass with fresh ice cubes and strain the drink into the glass. Top with soda water and stir. Garnish with a grapefruit wedge to serve.

TEQUILA SUNRISE

(Makes 1)

Tequila Sunrise—the name itself evokes a sense of ecstasy and joy. It's no coincidence that this was one of the most beloved cocktails of the 1970s—and it seems that perhaps the Rolling Stones are to blame. Legend says that the Tequila Sunrise originated at the Trident Hotel in Sausalito, California, during a private party for the Stones. Mick Jagger attempted to order a Margarita, but Bobby Lozoff, creator of the cocktail, offered him a Tequila Sunrise instead. The Stones embraced the drink so much that Keith Richards would later christen their 1972 tour, the "cocaine and Tequila Sunrise tour" in his autobiography, *Life*. In 1973, the Eagles would later go on to immortalize the Tequila Sunrise in a song of the same name. This cocktail is not only the epitome of rock and roll, it is also one of the easiest cocktails to make and enjoy.

Ingredients

2 fluid ounces blanco tequila
4 fluid ounces freshly squeezed orange juice
a dash of grenadine
an orange wedge and a cherry, to garnish

Instructions

Fill a collins glass with ice cubes, pour in the tequila and orange juice and stir. Pour in the grenadine in a slow, steady stream in the center of the drink and allow it to settle at the bottom, creating a gradient "sunrise" fade from red to orange. Garnish with an orange wedge and cherry and serve.

BLOODY MARIA

(Makes 1)

The Bloody Mary was created in the 1920s by Fernand Petiot, at Harry's New York Bar in Paris, where American expatriates and artists such as Ernest Hemingway and Salvador Dalí would frequently indulge in libations during the *années follies* (crazy years). The first version of this drink was made out of equal parts tomato juice and vodka, which had just arrived in the city alongside caviar and a population of refugees escaping the Russian Revolution. It is said to have been christened by two bar patrons from Chicago, who knew of a bar called Bucket of Blood, where there was a waitress named Mary. After taking the drink to the United States, Petiot added spices, Worcestershire sauce, and Tabasco to the mix. The drink's Mexican counterpart, the Bloody Maria, is made with tequila and is as legitimate as the original, adding a bit more character and vegetal earthiness to the mix, making it the perfect brunch drink.

Ingredients

2 fluid ounces reposado tequila
1 teaspoon drained bottled grated horseradish
3 dashes of Tabasco sauce
3 dashes of Worcestershire sauce
a dash of lime juice
3 dashes of salt
3 dashes of freshly ground black pepper
5 fluid ounces tomato juice
a lime wedge and a celery stalk, to garnish

Instructions

Mix all the ingredients, except the tomato juice and garnish, in a collins glass over ice and stir well. Top up with the tomato juice and stir again. Garnish with a lime wedge and a celery stalk and serve.

TEQUILA MOJITO

(Makes 1)

Originating in Cuba, the traditional Mojito was a humble attempt to mask the funky fierceness of cheap rum to make it more pleasing to the palate. And the mixture of lime, sugar, and mint makes for an addictive combination. Legend has it that Ernest Hemingway would drink his Mojitos with Champagne instead of soda water at the iconic Havana bar, La Bodeguita del Medio. We can only imagine what he would have thought of switching his rum for tequila. For mint-lovers and Margarita-lovers alike, the Tequila Mojito is the dream, bringing together two of the world's favorite cocktails into a mouthwatering pairing.

Ingredients

4 mint leaves
1 fluid ounce agave nectar
1 fluid ounce freshly squeezed lime juice
2 fluid ounces Herradura Blanco tequila
2 fluid ounces soda water

Instructions

Place the mint leaves, agave nectar, and lime juice in a collins glass. Mash the ingredients with a muddler or with the back of a spoon at the bottom of the glass. Next, fill the glass with ice cubes and add the tequila and soda water. Stir to blend.

MEZCAL MULE

(Makes 1)

It is said that the original Moscow Mule was invented to "clean out the basement." Like many other cocktails before it, the Mule was an accidental invention, created in an attempt to shift cases of Smirnoff vodka and ginger beer at a Manhattan bar in 1941. However, as soon as the first Mule was served, it was an instant success. Much like the incessant sharing of cocktail pics through Instagram today, the Moscow Mule's popularity spread like wildfire, aided by the invention of the Polaroid camera and a marketing genius by the name of John G. Martin, who would ask bartenders to pose with the cocktail served in a copper mug. Two pictures would be taken, one for the bartender to keep and display, and the other to show the next bar what the competition was doing. Swapping vodka for mezcal, and mixing the citrus notes of the agave with the spiciness and soothing qualities of the ginger beer, the Mezcal Mule is a very refreshing take on the 1940s classic.

Ingredients
2 fluid ounces espadín mezcal
¾ fluid ounce freshly squeezed lime juice
4 fluid ounces ginger beer
2 dashes of Angostura bitters
candied ginger, to garnish

Instructions
Add the mezcal, lime juice, ginger beer, and bitters to a collins glass filled with ice cubes and stir to mix. Garnish with a piece of candied ginger.

TEQUILA ZOMBIE

(Makes 1)

Pineapples, paper umbrellas, coconut cups, and curiously strong boozy drinks are all synonymous with Tiki. And while traditional Tiki drinks all include rum with a Polynesian flair, ultimately Tiki is a state of mind that pushes the boundaries of what you can imagine a cocktail to be. The Zombie, named after its supposed mind-altering effects, was created by Donn Beach of Hollywood's iconic Don the Beachcomber restaurant. This variation on the iconic classic adds both aged tequila and mezcal for extra earthiness and charm.

Ingredients
1 fluid ounce reposado tequila
½ fluid ounce aged Jamaican rum
½ fluid ounce espadín mezcal
¾ fluid ounce freshly squeezed lime juice
½ fluid ounce Velvet Falernum liqueur
½ fluid ounce Cinnamon Grapefruit Syrup (page 17)
1 teaspoon grenadine
a dash of Angostura bitters
a mint sprig, a grapefruit twist, a cherry, and
freshly grated cinnamon, to garnish

Instructions
Place all the ingredients, except the garnish, in a cocktail shaker and shake with 1 ice cube. Strain into a Tiki mug over crushed ice. Garnish with a mint sprig, grapefruit twist, cinnamon, and a cherry on top to serve.

MEZCAL OLD FASHIONED

(Makes 1)

Classic cocktails aren't always popular at their inception, but their simplicity and elegance mean they withstand the test of time. The classic—and delicious—Old Fashioned is often perceived as the "manliest" of cocktails to order. With this in mind, it seems appropriate to re-create it with one of the world's most audacious spirits: mezcal. You can tell a lot about a person from what they drink, but in this case, the simple nature of the Old Fashioned also reveals the character of the spirit within what is, quite possibly, one of the most expressive and elegant mezcal cocktails. After all, as Coco Chanel once said, "Simplicity is the keynote of all true elegance."

Ingredients
½ fluid ounce agave nectar
3-4 dashes of Angostura bitters
2 fluid ounces espadín mezcal
an orange peel twist, to garnish

Instructions
First, place a double rocks glass in the freezer or fill with ice cubes, tossing out once the glass is chilled. Place the agave nectar directly into the glass. Add the Angostura bitters and a large ice cube. Pour over the mezcal and stir well. Rub the rim of the glass with an orange peel twist and then drop it in the drink to serve.

FRIEND REQUEST

(Makes 1)

To accept or not to accept? Is that really the question?
In a world invaded by technology and a false sense of
connection, this is one friend request you simply won't want
to refuse. In this refreshing cocktail, bacanora—tequila and
mezcal's northern relative—invites you to be transported
to a place of bliss and revitalizing energy. Within the Friend
Request, bacanora and lime blend perfectly with the sweet
bubbles of the tonic to create a smooth, citric cocktail that
will feel like a cool summer breeze on your palate.

Ingredients

2 fluid ounces bacanora (or espadín mezcal)
¾ fluid ounce freshly squeezed lime juice
¾ fluid ounce Citrus Cordial (page 18)
2 fluid ounces tonic water
a lime twist, to garnish

Instructions

Pour all the liquid ingredients into a collins glass
over fresh ice cubes and stir to mix. Garnish with
a lime twist and paper straw to serve.

WHISKEY

90

BOURBON
WHISKEY

46% ALCOHOL 373 ML

aromatic bitters

ANGOSTURA

200 ml

FURIOSA

(Makes 1)

Named for Imperator Furiosa, one of the fiercest warriors
in the realm of the Mad Max saga, this is a knockout
cocktail that more than lives up to her name. Like Furiosa's
androgynous nature, mezcal and bourbon come together
with lime and ginger to balance the feminine and
masculine energy of each spirit. Add Angostura bitters
for effect, and you've got yourself a cocktail suitable for
the survival of humanity in a distant dystopian future.

Ingredients
1 fluid ounce espadín mezcal
1 fluid ounce bourbon
¾ fluid ounce freshly squeezed lemon juice
¾ fluid ounce Simple Syrup (page 17)
2 fluid ounces ginger beer
several dashes of Angostura bitters

Instructions
Fill a collins glass with fresh ice cubes, pour in all the
ingredients, except the bitters, and stir well. Add several
dashes of Angostura bitters and allow it to fade into the
drink, creating a gradient fade of color, and serve.

FOX FORCE FIVE

(Makes 1)

"It was a show about a team of female secret agents called 'Fox Force Five.' Fox, as in we're a bunch of foxy chicks. Force, as in we're a force to be reckoned with. Five, as in there's one ... two ... three ... four ... five of us."

This mighty cocktail is named after the infamous show in which "Mia Wallace" in *Pulp Fiction* (played by Uma Thurman) starred as one of five foxy female secret agents. It is a smashing blend of five ingredients: mezcal, Aperol, peach liqueur, pineapple, and lime. Each one is unique on its own, but, shaken together, a mighty force to be reckoned with.

Ingredients
1 ½ fluid ounces espadín mezcal
½ fluid ounce freshly squeezed pineapple juice
½ fluid ounce freshly squeezed lime juice
½ fluid ounce Aperol
¼ fluid ounce Giffard Crème de Pêche
¼ fluid ounce Simple Syrup (page 17)
1 fluid ounce sparkling water
a pineapple wedge, to garnish

Instructions
Place all the liquid ingredients, except the sparkling water, in a cocktail shaker with ice and shake. Strain into a hurricane glass filled with crushed ice. Top with sparkling water and garnish with a pineapple wedge.

BLOODY OAXACAN

(Makes 1)

Created at the posh restaurant, Anatol, in Polanco, Mexico City, this quenching cocktail is as satisfying as it is simple to mix. Prepare to indulge the way Mexico's top businesspeople, socialites, and politicians do when you try the Bloody Oaxacan. Known for its luxurious stores and busy bistros and terraces, Polanco is the place to be if you want to be seen in Mexico City. Combining the smokiness of mezcal with the sweetness of the fresh pineapple juice and a hint of hibiscus, the Bloody Oaxacan delivers an irresistible balance of sweet, smoky, and tart that will instantly transport you to a Sunday afternoon walking through the streets of one of Mexico City's most exclusive neighborhoods.

Ingredients
½ fluid ounce Hibiscus Tea (page 18)
2 fluid ounces espadín mezcal
1 fluid ounce Simple Syrup (page 17)
4 fluid ounces pineapple juice
a pineapple leaf, to garnish

Instructions
Brew hibiscus tea, according to the instructions on the packet (or page 18), prior to making the cocktail and allow it to cool. Place the mezcal, simple syrup, and pineapple juice in a cocktail shaker filled with ice and shake. Strain into a double rocks glass filled with ice cubes. Steadily pour the hibiscus tea into the center of the drink, allowing it to fade into the cocktail. Garnish with a pineapple leaf.

LUST FOR LIFE

(Makes 1)

As a product of its multicultural background, the history of mezcal in Mexico can be traced back to the 16th century, following the arrival of the Spaniards in Mesoamerica. The Lust for Life cocktail is the perfect example of how the fusion of two cultures can ultimately create something that enhances the qualities of each individual element. Old and New Worlds come together, as the espadín mezcal and sherry fuse with the sweet and acidic notes found in the pineapple, to create a refreshing but nutty and complex drink.

Ingredients
1 ½ fluid ounces espadín mezcal
¾ fluid ounce orgeat syrup (such as Torani)
¾ fluid ounce Palo Cortado sherry
½ fluid ounce freshly squeezed lemon juice
½ fluid ounce fresh pineapple juice

Instructions
Place all the ingredients in a cocktail shaker with ice. Shake and strain into a coupe glass.

LA CABRONA

(Makes 1)

Known as *La Doña*, María Félix remains a symbol of beauty, glamour, boldness, and independence. Her beautiful features captivated an entire generation during the Golden Age of Mexican cinema; however, her outspoken views and strong character have immortalized her as a fiercely bold and ambitious woman, despite living and working in an era dominated by men. Her *cabrona* (badass) attitude carved her place as an icon for women in Mexico and around the world. This cocktail is inspired by her legacy.

Ingredients
¾ fluid ounce freshly squeezed lime juice, plus extra for the rim
1½ fluid ounces espadín mezcal
¾ fluid ounce freshly squeezed blood orange juice
½ fluid ounce agave nectar
hibiscus salt, for the rim

Instructions
Moisten the rim of a double rocks glass with water or lime juice. Holding the glass upside down, dip the rim into the hibiscus salt. Place all the liquid ingredients in a cocktail shaker with ice and shake. Strain into the prepared glass over a large block of fresh ice.

EL BANDITO

(Makes 1)

WANTED. It's the end of spring and you're ready to transition into summer clothes, palm trees, and the sensation of the warm sun on your face. Spicy, smoky, and sweet, that's the Bandito, as the spiciness of Ancho Reyes tingles on the tip of your tongue while a wave of sweet tangy lime washes it away to leave you with a soothing, smoky finish. It's easy to say that one sip will leave you wanting more.

Ingredients
1 fluid ounce freshly squeezed lime juice, plus extra for the rim
1 fluid ounce Montelobos mezcal
1 fluid ounce Ancho Reyes chili liqueur
½ fluid ounce Simple Syrup (page 17)
salt, for the rim
a lime wheel and a mint sprig, to garnish

Instructions
Moisten the rim of a double rocks glass with water or lime juice. Holding the glass upside down, dip the rim into the salt. Place all the liquid ingredients in a cocktail shaker with ice and shake well. Strain and pour over fresh ice cubes into the prepared glass. Garnish with a lime wheel and mint sprig to serve.

32

EL BANDITO

LOBO NEGRO

(Makes 1)

The wolf is a symbol of the night. The often-misunderstood wolf is a fiercely loyal animal who, much like mezcal, is an undeterred free spirit. As a spirit animal, the lonesome wolf teaches us to take risks and discover our inner power and strength. The Lobo Negro cocktail, named after the rare black wolf, invites you to embrace your inner spirit animal. The smoky mezcal, combined with the spicy ginger syrup, brings out the sweet and earthy undertones of the blackberries for a cocktail that is not only delicious, but is also packed with antioxidants.

Ingredients
7 blackberries
2 fluid ounces Montelobos mezcal
1 ½ fluid ounces Ginger Syrup (page 18)
1 fluid ounce freshly squeezed lime juice

Instructions
Place 4 of the blackberries in a cocktail shaker and muddle. Add the rest of the ingredients to the shaker, add ice, and shake well to mix. Strain into a double rocks glass filled with fresh ice. Garnish with the remaining blackberries on a cocktail stick.

SICILIAN WOLF

(Makes 1)

The wolf has always played an important role in Italian mythology. As the founders of Rome, Romulus and Remus were nursed and sheltered by a she-wolf, considered sacred to devotees of the God of War, Mars. As a symbol of war, the apparition of a wolf before battle was considered good luck. In the modern age, catching sight of this Sicilian Wolf is believed to be a sign of good fortune. The blend of smoke, spice, and bitter in this delicious cocktail is all the liquid courage you'll need to face any endeavor.

Ingredients

1 ½ fluid ounces Montelobos mezcal
¾ fluid ounce Ancho Reyes chili liqueur
¾ fluid ounce Amaro Montenegro
½ fluid ounce Ginger Syrup (page 18)
½ fluid ounce yuzu juice (either found in a
   speciality store, or freshly squeezed)
½ fluid ounce freshly squeezed lime juice
an orange slice, to garnish

Instructions

Place all the ingredients, except the garnish, in a cocktail shaker filled with ice and shake well. Strain into a collins glass over fresh ice cubes. Garnish with an orange slice.

SMOKY DIABLO

(Makes 1)

"The path to paradise begins in hell."
Dante Alighieri

If ever there was a drink that could embody this quote, it would be the Smoky Diablo. When two protected designations of origin, or as the French would say, *appellation d'origine contrôlée*, meet—such as the savory Montelobos mezcal and fruity crème de cassis—the result is a potion that will instantly brighten your day—especially those gray, trying days when life really can feel like hell. With a bit of spicy ginger beer and lime, the Smoky Diablo will take you to paradise through a robust spicy and sweet journey of flavor.

Ingredients
2 fluid ounces Montelobos mezcal
4 fluid ounces ginger beer
½ fluid ounce freshly squeezed lime juice
¾ fluid ounce crème de cassis
a lime wheel and candied ginger, to garnish

Instructions
Pour the mezcal, ginger beer, and lime juice into a collins glass filled with ice. Lastly, pour the cassis along the inside of the glass and let it drizzle down the outside of the cocktail. Garnish with a lime wheel and candied ginger.

CAZUELITA

(Makes 4)

The Cazuelita embodies everything that is great about Mexican culture and tradition: family, flavor, and fun. Served in a traditional *cazuela de barro* (clay cooking pot), this cocktail is a concoction you could imagine any *abuelita* (grandmother) serving during a food-fueled family gathering. The Cazuelita includes one of Mexico's favorite ingredients: hibiscus. A hint of sweet and spice from the cinnamon syrup makes this the perfect punch bowl for your next party.

Ingredients
8 fluid ounces Hibiscus Tea (page 18)
4 fluid ounces Montelobos mezcal
1½ fluid ounces Cinnamon Syrup (such as Monin)
1½ fluid ounces freshly squeezed lime juice
cinnamon sticks and orange slices, to garnish

Instructions
Brew hibiscus tea, according to the instructions on the packet (or page 18), prior to making the cocktail. Place all the ingredients, except the garnish, in a small punch bowl and stir thoroughly. Add some ice cubes and garnish with floating cinnamon sticks and orange slices to serve. Ladle the drink into punch glasses.

CAFÉ AHUMADO

(Makes 1)

Adding a dash of alcohol to your freshly brewed coffee has traditionally been considered an Irish staple. However, add a little spice and smoke to the mix and you've got yourself a spiked version of a Mexican *café de olla*. In Mexico, coffee is anything but ordinary. Available at any hour of the day or night (as the name suggests), traditional *café de olla* is brewed in a clay pot, with cinnamon and *piloncillo* (unrefined whole cane sugar). Café Ahumado brings the celebrated Ancho Reyes to the mix, adding an extra layer of heat. Add mezcal and you have all the motivation you need to keep partying all night.

Ingredients
1 ½ fluid ounces Montelobos mezcal
¾ fluid ounce Ancho Reyes chili liqueur
4 fluid ounces freshly brewed hot coffee
2 dashes of Angostura bitters
grated orange zest and a cinnamon stick, to garnish

Instructions
Pour all the liquid ingredients into a heatproof coffee cup or mug and stir. Garnish with some grated orange zest on top and a cinnamon stick.

LA LOBA'S AGUA FRESCA

(Makes 1)

Sweet and refreshing, horchata is one of Mexico's favorite aguas frescas. Seen all over Mexico's markets and *taquerias* in large *vitroleros* (cylindrical glass containers) filled with ice, horchata is typically prepared with rice, vanilla, cinnamon, and occasionally condensed and evaporated milk. Without a doubt, this elixir is indispensable at any Mexican party, along with the also famous aguas de jamaica and tamarindo. La Loba's Agua Fresca, an elevated version of this thirst-quenching classic, is the perfect liquid fuel for any gathering.

Ingredients
1 ¼ fluid ounces Montelobos mezcal
1 fluid ounce Ancho Reyes chili liqueur
¾ fluid ounce orgeat syrup (such as Torani)
1 fluid ounce coconut milk
3 fluid ounces Horchata (Mexican rice water, page 18)
ground cinnamon and an edible flower, to garnish

Instructions
Pour all the liquid ingredients into a mixing glass over ice and stir. Using a cocktail sieve, strain and pour into a coconut shell (use a rocks glass if a shell is not available). Sprinkle cinnamon on top and garnish with an edible flower.

PREMIUM

AGAVE
NECTAR

1864

AZTEC
CHOCOLATE
BITTERS

TODDY OAXACAQUEÑO

(Makes 1)

The hot toddy is the drink of choice on a frosty winter's day. It is typically served as a combination of a base spirit (most commonly whisky), hot water, honey, and spices. Its roots can be traced back to Scottish tradition, where it was originally considered a cure for the common cold. Of course, like most drinks that originated as ailment relief, this now-popular cocktail has become a staple of fall and winter menus at bars all over the world. In this embodiment of the classic toddy, Aztec spices and flavors are fused with the citric essence of quintessential English tea.

Ingredients

4 fluid ounces freshly brewed Earl Grey tea, hot and strong
1 ½ fluid ounces Montelobos mezcal
½ fluid ounce agave nectar
2 dashes of Aztec chocolate bitters
½ fluid ounce freshly squeezed lemon juice
an orange slice and a piece of dark chocolate, to garnish

Instructions

Brew Earl Grey tea, and steep for 5 minutes, prior to making the cocktail. (For a stronger flavor, add more tea, not more time.) Place the mezcal, hot tea, agave nectar, bitters, and lemon juice in a heatproof mug. Stir well and garnish with the orange slice and dark chocolate on the side.

SPANISH MILK PUNCH

(Makes 1)

Clarified milk punch, also called English milk punch, is a classic early cocktail that can be traced as far back as the 17th century. The clarification process is a very old technique that was used to stabilize and preserve the punch, as well as to smooth out the harsh flavor of the rougher alcohol available at the time. The result is a clear, silky, almost milky drink with a mellow flavor. This punch is the perfect concoction to prepare in advance for your next holiday party, or to keep stored in your refrigerator for a post-work tipple. This recipe takes 3 days to prepare, but it is definitely worth the work.

Ingredients

6 pineapples, diced
peel of 5 oranges
6 cups granulated sugar
5 thyme sprigs
4 cinnamon sticks
7 whole star anise
21 fluid ounces freshly squeezed lime juice
21 fluid ounces espadín mezcal
12 fluid ounces Avua Prata Cachaça
12 fluid ounces Avión Silver tequila
8 fluid ounces white Rhum Agricole
3 fluid ounces Pernod Absinthe
3 fluid ounces Giffard Ginger liqueur of the Indies
2.5 quarts English Breakfast black tea
21 fluid ounces whole milk
orange slices, to garnish

Instructions

Day 1

Place the diced pineapple, orange peel, and sugar in a large, clear (ideally lidded) container and muddle together into a purée. To the mixture, add the thyme, cinnamon, and star anise. Pour in the lime juice, mezcal, cachaça, tequila, rum, absinthe, and Giffard. Add the black tea. Refrigerate and leave it to infuse overnight (24 hours).

Day 2

Remove the mixture from the refrigerator and strain the batch through a fine-mesh sieve into another clear container. Boil the milk, add to the container, and observe how the lactic acid solidifies. With a julep strainer, scoop out the curdled milk. Pass the concoction through the fine sieve again until you have a cloudy solution. Seal the container and place in the refrigerator, leaving it to rest for another 24 hours.

Day 3

Remove your container from the refrigerator. Now that the residual milk has settled to the bottom of the container, carefully tilt the container and pour the clear product into another large vessel, such as a punch bowl. Serve the clear liquid in a large punch bowl and garnish with floating orange slices. Serve by ladling into ice-filled double rocks glasses.

PECHUGA TONIC

(Makes 1)

It's the beginning of spring, and with longer days, sunshine, and new blooms comes the promise of thirst-quenching boozy tonics. The ever-so-popular Gin and Tonic gets revamped in this celebratory version with Pechuga mezcal. The history of the Mezcal de Pechuga in Santiago Matatlan can be traced back to 1930, when a stranger from Rio Seco migrated to the town. It is said that when a group of musicians came to the village, he held a reception in their honor and handed the leader a bottle of Pechuga. Many imbibed the spirit for the first time and, captivated by its sophisticated and unique flavors, it soon became the spirit of choice for celebratory occasions. The distillation of espadín mezcal with tropical fruits and spices, including tejocote, guava, pineapple, apples, cinnamon, and clove, turns this particular mezcal into the perfect gin substitute. Add a sprig of thyme, or a peel of grapefruit or kaffir lime, and serve it in a big stemmed wine goblet, transforming your Pechuga Tonic into the perfect spring drink.

Ingredients

4 fluid ounces Fever Tree tonic water
2 fluid ounces Pechuga mezcal
1 slice of grapefruit or kaffir lime, to garnish
salt

Instructions

Pour the tonic water and mezcal into a stemmed wine goblet filled with ice and stir. Garnish with a grapefruit or lime slice and dust the top of the cocktail lightly with kosher salt.

TEQUILA SHRUB

(Makes 1)

A shrub is a concentrated syrup made up of fruit, sugar, and vinegar. Shrubs are often used in cocktails mixed with spirits or on their own with soda water to create interesting flavor combinations that are also healthy.* This tequila shrub combines the diuretic properties of hibiscus with the antioxidants found in blackberries, to create a tangy cocktail packed with flavor and health benefits.

*Of course, while alcohol's traits of deliciousness and fun times are also a benefit, they cannot be counted as a health benefit… But that's what your vitamins are for!

Ingredients
2 fluid ounces añejo tequila
1 fluid ounce Hibiscus Syrup (page 19)
1½ fluid ounces Blackberry Vinaigrette (page 19)
¼ fluid ounce freshly squeezed lemon juice
½ fluid ounce sweet vermouth
a lemon slice, 3 blackberries, and a basil leaf, to garnish

Instructions
Place all the ingredients, except the garnish, in a cocktail shaker filled with ice and shake. Strain into a double rocks glass filled with crushed ice. Garnish with a lemon slice, 3 blackberries, and a basil leaf.

PRODUCT OF
SONORA
MEXICO

BACANORA

FIRE ON THE MOUNTAIN

(Makes 1)

As tequila and mezcal's fiery agave cousin, the desert-mountain terroir of bacanora is highlighted in this twist on the classic Negroni. The warm, arid terrain of the Sonoran Desert is brought to life in Fire on the Mountain, as the notes of tobacco and leather found in the bacanora are accentuated by the vanilla, caramel, and licorice flavors of the Carpana Antica vermouth. Add a bitter element and you have the perfect aperitif to kick off happy hour. Swap the bacanora for mezcal for a smokier version, or añejo or reposado tequila for a more vegetal, nutty flavor.

Ingredients
1 ½ fluid ounces bacanora (or tequila or mezcal)
¾ fluid ounce Leopold Bros Aperitivo
¾ fluid ounce Carpano Antica vermouth
a small twist of blood orange peel, to garnish

Instructions
Start by chilling a coupe glass in the freezer, or by filling it with ice, tossing the ice out once the glass is frosted. Add all the ingredients, except the garnish, to a mixing glass or jug and stir well. Strain into the chilled glass and garnish with the blood orange peel.

PACIFIC STANDARD

(Makes 1)

Beautiful weather, a vacation paradise, and the best sunsets.
The saying goes that the "West Coast is the Best Coast," and
the Pacific truly is paradise. When you live your life according
to Pacific Standard Time, you get the best of everything
life can offer, and this cocktail delivers it all in one simple
drink. One sip of the Pacific Standard and you'll be packing
your bags for California, without ever looking back. And if
traveling to a different time zone is made impossible by the
comings and goings of everyday life, remember it's always
happy hour somewhere.

Ingredients

1 ½ fluid ounces Altos Plata tequila
1 fluid ounce Aperol
¾ fluid ounce Carpano Antica vermouth
1 bar spoon Green Chartreuse
a flamed orange peel, to garnish

Instructions

Start by chilling a coupe glass, or a Nick and Nora glass,
in the freezer, or by filling the glass with ice, tossing it out
once the glass is frosted. (Halfway between a coupe
and a wine glass, the Nick and Nora glass is making a
comeback among cocktail-makers in the know.) Add all
the ingredients, except the garnish, to a mixing glass filled
with ice and stir well. Strain and serve in the chilled glass.

CHARTREUSE

LIQUEUR FABRIQUÉE
PAR LES PERES   CHARTREUX

1605   L. Garnier

Product of France

ALC 40% BY VOL   750 ML

CHARTREUSE DIFFUSION

APEROL

Aperitivo
LIQUER

ITALY

A

BARBIERI

AGAVE BRAVO

(Makes 1)

With three different presentations of agave, it's no wonder this cocktail is called the Agave Bravo. This triple-agave concoction is another variation of the standard classic, the Old Fashioned. Served with reposado tequila, espadín mezcal, agave nectar, and orange bitters, this simple recipe takes center stage as one of the best stirred agave cocktails. Just add a dash of orange bitters to tie in the nutty notes of the oak-aged tequila with the smokiness of the mezcal.

Ingredients
1 ½ fluid ounces Fortaleza reposado tequila
¼ fluid ounce agave nectar
a dash of orange bitters
½ fluid ounce espadín mezcal
a piece of grapefruit peel, to garnish

Instructions
First, place a coupe glass in the freezer, or fill with ice to chill, tossing out the ice once the glass is cold. Place the tequila, agave nectar, and bitters in a mixing glass filled with ice and stir well. Strain into the chilled glass, then top up with the mezcal to create a separate layer on top. Garnish with grapefruit peel to serve.

SIN NOMBRE

(Makes 1)

Just like the various anonymous agave spirits from Tequila or Oaxaca that are bottled in unbranded Coca-Cola or water bottles, this cocktail needs neither introduction nor label. It can stand on its own, thanks to its unique ingredients, with no need for branding. The moment the fizzy bubbles of Prosecco, alongside the lime and the earthy, vegetal complexity of the blanco tequila, touch the tip of your tongue, you will want to remain anonymous to drink these all night without anybody noticing. No need to call it by its name, one sip of this cocktail and you'll be able to see right through it.

Ingredients
1 ½ fluid ounces Fortaleza blanco tequila
⅜ fluid ounce maraschino liqueur
¾ fluid ounce freshly squeezed lime juice
⅜ fluid ounce Simple Syrup (page 17)
a dash of lime bitters
2 fluid ounces Prosecco
salt and a lime wheel, to garnish

Instructions
Place the tequila, maraschino liqueur, lime juice, syrup, and bitters in a cocktail shaker filled with ice and shake. Strain into a collins glass filled with ice cubes and sprinkle salt on top. Top up with the Prosecco (causing the salt to mix in) and garnish with a lime wheel to serve.

it's always sunny!

MEXICO

hola.

YUM!

wish you
were here!   X

R. PARKER
9 HOME STREET
LONDON
SE16 V   UK

PENCIL

IT'S ALWAYS SUNNY

(Makes 1)

Those who have traveled to Cuernavaca, the setting for
Malcolm Lowry's novel *Under the Volcano*, know that it's
always sunny in the city of the eternal spring. Bursting
with the constant blossom of *bugambilias* (bougainvillea),
Cuernavaca is the vacation town of choice for all the
capitalinos, or inhabitants of the great metropolis of Mexico
City. Like the colorful city itself, this cocktail embodies the
charm of an ever-blooming town that is ensconced by two
majestic volcanos.

Ingredients
1 ½ fluid ounces Fortaleza reposado tequila
½ fluid ounce freshly squeezed lemon juice
½ fluid ounce freshly squeezed orange juice
½ fluid ounce Simple Syrup (page 17)
2 dashes of Angostura bitters
½ fluid ounce Pierre Ferrand Dry Curaçao
ginger beer, to top up
a twist of orange peel, to garnish

Instructions
First, chill a coupe glass by placing it in the freezer or filling it
with ice cubes, tossing them out once the glass is chilled. Add
the tequila, lemon juice, orange juice, simple syrup, bitters, and
Curaçao to a cocktail shaker filled with ice and shake. Strain
into the chilled glass. Top up with a splash of ginger beer and
garnish with orange peel to serve.

LITTLE REGRET

(Makes 1)

Tepache is a traditional Mexican beverage made from the fermented skin and pulp of the pineapple. Much like pulque, its origins are pre-Hispanic and it is ideal for sipping on a hot summer's day. Much like the day the Little Regret was conceived. Picture an eroding trail descending onto a beautiful, secluded beach with sea stacks, caves, and arched rocks along the shore. A school of mermaids sits upon the sand, laughing carelessly without regrets as the sun begins to set on another day. That's how this cocktail, a pineapple variation of the Paloma Classic (page 56), will make you feel with every sip. Because after all, life is too short to wake up in the morning with regrets.

Ingredients
1½ fluid ounces Regret Shrub (page 19)
1½ fluid ounces espadín mezcal
Tepache (page 20) or pineapple cider, to top up
a pineapple wedge, to garnish

Instructions
First, chill a coupe glass by placing it in the freezer or filling it with ice cubes, tossing them out once the glass is cold. Place the shrub and mezcal in a cocktail shaker with ice and shake lightly. Strain into the prepared glass and top with the tepache. Garnish with a pineapple wedge.

LEVITATION
(Makes 1)

The Levitation cocktail is a spin-off of the Margarita, but with gin at center stage. The botanical fragrance of the gin, combined with the vegetal notes of the jalapeño and mezcal, gives this cocktail a spicy and refreshing mouthfeel that will make you feel warm and cool at the same time. Add lemon juice and the sweetness of maraschino liqueur to create the perfectly balanced cocktail, ideal for sipping on a warm day that transforms into a cool summer night.

Ingredients
½ fluid ounce Luxardo maraschino liqueur
2 slices of jalapeño (with seeds removed)
1 fluid ounce Plymouth gin
½ fluid ounce espadín mezcal
¾ fluid ounce freshly squeezed lemon juice

Instructions
Place all the ingredients, including one slice of jalapeño, in a cocktail shaker filled with ice and shake. Strain into a double rocks glass with one large ice cube and garnish with a jalapeño slice.

LOCAL CELEBRITY

(Makes 1)

Well known at the local watering hole but a complete unknown everywhere else. Here's a taste of something unexpected. The Local Celebrity emanates the essence of a well-known Negroni, while at the same time embodying the personality of an eccentric spirit accentuated by the bitterness of an Amaro and the bright-orange flavor of Aperol. Whether it's the Local Celebrity's first appearance or a common recurrence, this cocktail is sure to make an impression with everyone at your next social gathering.

Ingredients

1 fluid ounce espadín mezcal
1 fluid ounce Amaro Montenegro
½ fluid ounce Aperol
½ fluid ounce Contratto Bianco vermouth (or Lillet)
a twist of orange peel, to garnish

Instructions

Place all the ingredients, except the garnish, in a mixing glass and stir well. Strain into a coupe glass or a Nick and Nora glass. (Halfway between a coupe and a wine glass, the Nick and Nora glass is making a comeback among cocktail-makers in the know.) Garnish with the orange peel and serve.

TEQUILA JULEP

(Makes 1)

Amid a celebration of Southern pride, over 120,000 Bourbon Mint Juleps are made during the annual Kentucky Derby, served to horse aficionados in traditional pewter cups overfilled with crushed ice as the staple of the world-famous race. The word "julep" is derived from the Persian *gulab*, denoting sweetened rose water. The word crossed over to Arabic as *julab* and later *julapium* in Latin. Eventually, a julep came to be known as a medicinal syrup, flavored with herbal essences. Before the Mint Julep became the favorite cocktail of the South, it was seen as a restorative tonic that would invigorate farmers before they would step out into the fields each morning. This julep, made with aged tequila and served in a copper mug, is a south-of-the-border version perfect for any warm summer evening.

Ingredients

5 mint sprigs
¾ fluid ounce agave nectar
2 fluid ounces añejo tequila

Instructions

Muddle 4 of the mint sprigs in the bottom of a julep cup (a copper or pewter mug is recommended). Add the agave nectar and a bar spoon of water. Fill the cup with crushed ice. Add the tequila and stir well. Garnish with the remaining mint sprig.

EL AVENTURERO

(Makes 1)

Watch out, girls; El Aventurero is here. He does what he wants; he is humble and a good friend. Funny and sincere. He plays cards and knows how to party. He drinks both tequila and mezcal, pulque and Champagne. Named after the song made famous by Antonio Aguilar, El Aventurero embodies everything that is Mexican charm. The añejo tequila, jalapeño, and the tartness of lime and fruitiness of pomegranate will keep you wanting more.

Ingredients

1 ½ fluid ounces añejo tequila
½ fluid ounce Jalapeño Simple Syrup (page 20)
1 fluid ounce freshly squeezed lime juice
1 fluid ounce 100% pure pomegranate juice

Instructions

Place all the ingredients in a cocktail shaker filled with ice and shake well. Strain into a vintage, stemmed cocktail glass and serve.

MEXICAN DELIGHT

(Makes 1)

If you've ever read C. S. Lewis' *The Lion, The Witch and The Wardrobe*, you know the infamous story of how Edmund gives up his brothers and sisters to the wicked witch in exchange for a box of Turkish Delight. After having a sip of this Mexican Delight, you will surely give up not only your siblings, but your *mamacita* and *papacito* as well. This combination of tequila and yellow Chartreuse is enough to make you go mad for a bit more of that Mexican delight.

Ingredients
1 ½ fluid ounces reposado tequila
½ fluid ounce yellow Chartreuse
1 fluid ounce pineapple juice
1 fluid ounce freshly squeezed lime juice
½ fluid ounce agave nectar
a lime wheel and an edible flower (such
   as a nasturtium), to garnish

Instructions
Place all the liquid ingredients in a cocktail shaker filled with ice and shake. Strain over fresh ice into a stemmed wine glass. Garnish with a lime wheel and an edible flower to serve.

LA CURA

(Makes 4)

Legend has it that in 1930, an influenza epidemic hit northern Mexico. The best medicine for it? Tequila, of course. A Monterrey doctor from this legend, believing he had avoided contagion due to his daily lunchtime shot of tequila with salt and lime, prescribed this remedy to all his patients. And there began the custom of sipping tequila with salt and lime. In this hydrating version of the original remedy, add coconut water and agave nectar to enhance the healing properties of the tequila.

Ingredients

freshly squeezed juice of 2 limes, plus extra for the rim
4 fluid ounces blanco tequila
2 tablespoons agave nectar
3 fluid ounces coconut water
½–1 cup of ice
coconut flakes, for the rim

Instructions

Moisten the rim of 4 shot glasses with water or lime juice. Holding the glasses upside down, dip the rim into the coconut flakes. Place the tequila, lime juice, agave nectar, coconut water, and ice in a cocktail shaker, and shake. Strain into the shot glasses and serve.

STRAWBERRY TEQUILA SOUR

(Makes 1)

Synonymous with summer, the arrival of strawberry season will gain new meaning after you've tried this fruity Tequila Sour. There is no better way to kick off summertime than with this delectable concoction in which agave and strawberries go hand-in-hand, creating a frothy, sweet, and light cocktail. The Strawberry Tequila Sour is practically dessert in a glass, reminiscent of a fresh strawberry lemon meringue pie—but it's easy to make and with fewer calories!

Ingredients
2 fluid ounces blanco tequila
3 strawberries, chopped, plus an extra strawberry to garnish
1 teaspoon agave nectar
juice of ½ lemon
1 egg white
a dash of Angostura bitters, to garnish

Instructions
First, chill a coupe glass by leaving it in the freezer or filling it with ice cubes, tossing them out once the glass is cold. To a cocktail shaker, add the tequila, strawberries, agave nectar, lemon juice, and egg white. Dry shake (without ice) for 20 seconds, then add ½ cup of ice and shake again for 10 seconds. Strain into the chilled glass. Garnish with a strawberry and a dash of Angostura bitters to serve.

GRILLED PINEAPPLE & MINT TEQUILA LEMONADE

(Makes 1)

We all know the saying: when life gives you lemons, make lemonade. But when life also gives you pineapple and mint, then find a friend whose life has given them tequila and throw a party! This lemonade is a far cry from the fizzy drink known in the U.K. An upgraded version of the American summer classic, this blend of grilled pineapple, mint, and reposado tequila will leave your neighbors wishing you would set up a lemonade stand.

Ingredients

3 slices of grilled pineapple, chopped, plus extra to garnish
5 mint leaves, chopped, plus extra to garnish
1½ fluid ounces reposado tequila
4–6 fluid ounces still, "American-style" lemonade
1 teaspoon agave nectar

Instructions

Prior to making the cocktail, remove the skin of a fresh pineapple and cut into thick slices (about 1 inch). Preheat a grill to high and lightly oil the grate or rack. Grill for 2 to 3 minutes per side, or until lightly golden brown with grill marks. Allow to cool before adding to your drink. Place the grilled pineapple, mint leaves, and tequila (keeping back extra pineapple and mint for garnish) in the bottom of a cocktail shaker and muddle. Add a cup of ice, agave nectar, and lemonade and shake well. Strain into a double rocks glass filled with fresh ice cubes. Garnish with a grilled pineapple slice and mint to serve.

TEQUILA 100% AGAVE REPOSADO

TEQUILA NEGRONI SOUR

(Makes 1)

Sours are not only delightful to drink; the preparation is a spectacle, too. Spend enough time propping up a bar, and eventually you'll overhear a voice asking why in the world an egg is being added to their cocktail. Egg whites: The secret to adding richness and texture to a cocktail. The simple egg white's first official appearance was in the Whiskey Sour in Jerry Thomas's *Bartender's Guide* as early as 1862. We've come a long way since then, and in this twist on the classic, Campari and sweet vermouth are added to the tequila for extra drama. To properly enjoy this deliciously rich and bitter cocktail, be sure to use only fresh, washed eggs.

Ingredients

1½ fluid ounces reposado tequila
1 fluid ounce Campari
1 fluid ounce sweet vermouth
1 teaspoon agave nectar
juice of ½ lemon
1 egg white
a thyme sprig, to garnish

Instructions

First, chill a coupe glass by leaving it in the freezer or filling it with ice cubes, tossing them out once the glass is cold. Place the tequila, Campari, vermouth, agave nectar, lemon juice, and egg white in a cocktail shaker. Dry shake (without ice) for 20 seconds, then add ice and shake again. Strain into the coupe glass and garnish with a thyme sprig to serve.

PEPE COLLINS

(Makes 1)

The traditional Collins cocktail is that all-around good guy who fits every occasion. An everyday sipper and easy to make at the drop of a hat, the Pepe is the Mexican cousin of the Tom Collins, and is as refreshing as it is tasty. But as simple as it is to make, quality is key. Be sure to use your favorite tequila and not to skimp on quality, as it will be the star of the show in this icy cocktail, sure to become your new go-to drink.

Ingredients

1 ½ fluid ounces reposado tequila
1 fluid ounce freshly squeezed lemon juice
½ fluid ounce agave nectar
2 fluid ounces soda water
a lemon wedge, to garnish

Instructions

Pour the tequila, lemon juice, and agave nectar into a collins glass filled with ice cubes. Stir thoroughly. Top with the soda water and garnish with a lemon wedge.

SPLASHBACK

(Makes 1)

When it comes to modifiers that mix well with mezcal, there is no need to look further than Campari. And far more than simply the Negroni's perfect sidekick, Campari is also mezcal's best friend when it comes to creating stimulating cocktails. Something bitter, something sour, something smoky? The Splashback has something for everyone, with this bright and juicy concoction. Serve this at your next summer party and be ready to make some waves.

Ingredients

2 fluid ounces espadín mezcal

1 fluid ounce Campari

1 fluid ounce passionfruit juice

1 fluid ounce freshly squeezed lime juice

a twist of lime, to garnish

Instructions

Place all the ingredients, except the garnish, in a cocktail shaker filled with ice. Shake well and strain into a double rocks glass filled with fresh ice cubes. Garnish with a twist of lime to serve.

DISCO & VINE

(Makes 1)

This glam version of the popular Sex on the Beach cocktail lends a cool Baja vibe to the beloved summer classic. Named after the famous '70s era of glam—and one of the most famous cross streets of Hollywood Boulevard— the Disco & Vine is sure to become your next party cocktail. Swapping vodka for tequila, the Disco & Vine's watermelon-and-aloe combination makes it the perfect cocktail to be sipped poolside or on the dance floor.

Ingredients

1¾ fluid ounces reposado tequila
½ fluid ounce Chareau aloe liqueur (or aloe vera juice)
½ fluid ounce Orange and Saffron Syrup (page 20)
½ fluid ounce freshly squeezed watermelon juice
½ fluid ounce freshly squeezed lemon juice
a watermelon slice and chili powder, to garnish
a pinch of sea salt

Instructions

Place the tequila, aloe, syrup, watermelon juice, and lemon juice in a cocktail shaker filled with ice. Shake and strain into a collins glass filled with ice cubes. Garnish with a watermelon slice dusted in chili powder to serve. Sprinkle sea salt on top for extra flavor.

INDEX

142

CREDITS

Cecilia Rios Murrieta would like to thank:

My editor Caitlin Doyle, for her incredible patience, kindness, and guidance through the process of writing my first book. You made me look deeper into something that is very near and dear to my heart and made me fall in love all over again with agave. Thank you. You and I need to sit down and share some mezcals together.

Ulises Torrentera, the Mexican Lowry, for believing in me and genuinely supporting me and teaching me about the mysticism behind the spirits we share and love. Every agave lover owes you a great deal for the passion you have shared and ignited within us.

My cocktail contributors, without whom this book would practically be nonexistent. Thank you, Jaymee Mandeville, "La Loba" Camille Austin, Cabell Thompson, Amanda Gunderson, Karl Steuck, Natalie Migliarini, Darwin Pornell, Yael Vengroff, Aaron Polsky, Emily Mistell, Lainey Collum, Cocktail Academy, Katy O'Donnell, Edwin Osegueda, Alejandro Blanco, and Antonio Barroeta for sharing your wonderful creations with everyone. I raise my mezcal to you!

Lili Murrieta, Carolina Saracho, Alicia Catelli, Jen Len, Daniel, and Vanessa Elkins—for being my biggest supporters and greatest critics. I promise to one day repay all the kind gestures and words of support you have shared with me throughout my journey. In the meantime, you will all have unlimited access to mezcal.

My brother Luis, and my mother and father, for never ceasing to believe in me.

Ruby Taylor would like to thank:

For all the love, support (and drinks) always;
Katie Price, Nancy Edmondson, Billie Alder,
Ella Antebi, Roxanne Simmonds, Pema
Seely, Ellie Yates, Anita Kershaw.